Standing in a Governor's Shoes

Ryan Nagelhout

Cavendish
Square

New York

Published in 2016 by Cavendish Square Publishing, LLC
243 5th Avenue, Suite 136, New York, NY 10016

Copyright © 2016 by Cavendish Square Publishing, LLC

First Edition

Website: cavendishsq.com

This publication represents the opinions and views of the author based on his or her personal experience, knowledge, and research. The information in this book serves as a general guide only. The author and publisher have used their best efforts in preparing this book and disclaim liability rising directly or indirectly from the use and application of this book.

CPSIA Compliance Information: Batch #WS15CSQ

All websites were available and accurate when this book was sent to press.

Library of Congress Cataloging-in-Publication Data

Nagelhout, Ryan.
Standing in a governor's shoes / Ryan Nagelhout.
pages cm. — (My government)
Includes bibliographical references and index.
ISBN 978-1-50260-476-7 (hardcover) ISBN 978-1-50260-475-0 (paperback) ISBN 978-1-50260-477-4 (ebook)
1. Governors—United States—Juvenile literature. 2. State governments—United States—Juvenile literature. I. Title.

JK2447.N35 2016
352.23'2130973—dc23

2015011251

Editorial Director: David McNamara
Editor: Amy Hayes
Copy Editor: Cynthia Roby
Art Director: Jeffrey Talbot
Designer: Alan Sliwinski
Senior Production Manager: Jennifer Ryder-Talbot
Production Editor: Renni Johnson
Photo Research: J8 Media

The photographs in this book are used by permission and through the courtesy of: Goodcat/Shutterstock.com, cover; Willowpix/iStockphoto.com, 4; Becky Bohrer/AP Images, 6; Public domain/Miles530/File:Iowa Senate.jpg/Wikimedia Commons, 8; Spencer Platt/Getty Images, 9; Jay Janner/Austin American-Statesman/AP Images, 10; Nagel Photography/Shutterstock.com, 12; Jonathan Wiggs/The Boston Globe/Getty Images, 15; Win McNamee/Getty Images, 17; John Gress/Getty Images, 18; Alex Wong/Getty Images, 20; Scott Eells/Bloomberg/Getty Images, 23; Rena Schild/Shutterstock.com, 24; Blend Images/Shutterstock.com, 26; Trekandshoot/Shutterstock.com, 27.

Printed in the United States of America

TABLE OF CONTENTS

FOUNDED 1634

MARYLAND
WELCOMES YOU

ENJOY YOUR VISIT!

Martin O'Malley
Governor

Many states list their governor on signs
you can see while traveling on highways.

The organization of the United States government can be hard to understand at times. Each part works together in some way, but it can be difficult to know who is in charge. The head of the **federal** government is the president. But who gets to run the state or territory where you live? There are many different elected officials, from state **legislatures** to city mayors. The leader of a state government, however, is called a governor.

There are a total of fifty-five governors in the United States. But if there are fifty states in the country, what do those five other governors do? Their job is to govern territories such as Guam and Puerto Rico.

Each of the fifty states is very different. This means that no two governors have the same responsibilities and expectations in office.

CHAPTER ONE

The Responsibilities of a Governor

The head of each state and territory may share the same title, but no two governors are alike. Each has different responsibilities as governor. States have their own **constitutions** that lay out how a state's government will work. The state constitution also sets the rules a governor must follow.

The rules that determine who can be governor are often different in each state. Governors need to be citizens of the United States, but each state may have more specific rules. Some rules require people to have lived in the state for a certain amount of time before they can run for office. This is called a residency rule.

Governors involved with making state laws may spend lots of time debating bills in state senate chambers.

Some states have age requirements. In New Hampshire, for example, you must be at least thirty years old to run for governor. In California, you must be eighteen years old and a registered voter. Some other states, such as Kansas and Vermont, have no age requirements.

Most governors serve four-year terms. However, some states, such as New Hampshire and Vermont, only have two-year terms. State constitutions also limit how many terms you can serve as governor. In some states, such as California, governors can only serve two terms. In many other states, the governor can keep serving as long as he or she keeps winning elections.

What governors can actually do also depends on the state they **represent**. At the very least, they can **influence** public opinion on issues that concern the state. Governors give speeches before voters as well as the legislature. Some states, such as New York, have governors deliver a State of

A State of the State address serves to update lawmakers and citizens on what the state government wants to accomplish in the coming year.

The governor and lieutenant governor often work together to run the state. Each lieutenant governor has different responsibilities.

the State address. This is similar to the State of the Union address the president gives the nation each year.

The **veto** is one of the most important parts of a governor's powers. All fifty state governors can veto bills passed by state legislatures. Governors can also support, or sponsor, laws, bringing them to the state legislature to vote on. State governors also direct the state's military. They can declare a state of emergency if bad weather or other events occur in the state.

Every governor has a different level of power. Some states, such as New York, have a strong governor who is responsible for the state budget and **appointing** people to positions in the state government that are vacant. Other states limit the powers of a governor and don't allow them to appoint many people to offices.

Texas is one of the states where the governor does not have a lot of power. In fact, the lieutenant governor of Texas is often seen as more powerful than the governor! The governor's budget is usually ignored, while the lieutenant governor controls the flow of bills to the floor of the state senate and appoints people to senate committees, or groups.

Walking in the Governor's Shoes

All five territory governors are men. Only thirty-five women have served as governor throughout United States history. Four came into their position through succession, without being officially elected.

Many states have a large house called the governor's mansion.
Once elected, governors can choose to live there with their families.

CHAPTER TWO

Governor for a Day

Each day is full of important responsibilities for governors. Many travel across their state to attend events, give speeches, and meet with people to discuss important issues. Your state's governor may post his or her daily schedule online. With a schedule, you can track what he or she does each day. So, what does a typical day look like for a governor?

MORNING

A governor usually starts his or her day in the state capitol. Some governors live in their own homes, while others stay in the governor's **mansion**. They usually wake up early and

Walking in the Governor's Shoes

Many governors today don't live in their state's governor's mansion. They believe that staying in their own homes can save the state money. There are only six states that don't have a governor's mansion.

have breakfast while reviewing the day's planned schedule. Some like to catch up on current events by reading newspapers or surfing the Internet.

Many governors schedule media events for the mornings. They are guests on radio shows and answer questions from concerned residents of their state. They sometimes make appearances on television news programs, where they discuss important state-related issues.

AFTERNOON

Every day, governors have meetings with many different people in the capitol. They often meet with their cabinet, or a group of people who help them in making decisions about different issues. Sometimes they will come together over lunch and discuss different projects they are working on, such as bills or the budget.

If a governor is traveling around the state, he or she may spend afternoons visiting schools, factories, or other government buildings. During these visits, the governor is updated on programs that the state pays for using taxpayer money. Governors need to make sure they are supporting programs that help people find jobs, get a good education, and keep them safe.

Visiting people around the state gives governors a better idea of what's important to citizens and how they live.

Walking in the Governor's Shoes

Many governors join the National Governors **Association**. This is a group of governors who work together to discuss the government and help decide the role they should play in politics. They often meet in Washington, DC, with people in other areas of government.

EVENING

When a governor is in the state capital, he or she might attend special events in the evening. When a governor travels to Washington, DC, he or she meets with other federal officials. A governor also visits local leaders when traveling throughout his or her state.

Talking to the print and online media is also a big part of a governor's job. He or she may give statements and take questions from media representatives. This is called a press conference. New government programs are often announced during these conferences. Some governors host regular press conferences to update the media on projects they are working on.

Governors often spend time together in Washington, DC. There they meet with federal leaders to help causes in their states.

After a long day, governors like to relax. Some spend time with their family at home. They may attend baseball games or go to the theater. They may be in charge of your state, but governors have hobbies, too!

Walking in the Governor's Shoes

Many early state governors became major figures in United States history. The second governor of Virginia was Thomas Jefferson. He wrote the **Declaration of Independence** and later became president of the United States.

BRING BACK ILLINOIS

Campaigning for governor can be a long,
tough test of a person's beliefs and goals.

Paid for by Citizens for Rauner, Inc.

CHAPTER THREE

How Does One Become a Governor?

Most governors held other government jobs before being elected to their current position. They may have served as the mayor of a city, a representative in a state legislature, or as a representative or senator in congress.

Before getting involved in politics, a potential governor is expected have a high school diploma. Many future governors also attend college and study law, political science, or other topics that help them understand how the government works.

Governors who work together while in office often support one another and help each other raise money during election season.

Many of the territory governors have lived in their territories their entire lives and have helped represent their home in the federal government. Lolo Matalasi Moliga became governor of American Samoa after serving eight years for the territory in the House of Representatives. Before that, he was a principal at a high school!

Someone who wants to be governor needs to be elected into office by the people. This means that they have to **campaign** for the office. Campaigning for governor can be a long and expensive process. A candidate must travel around the state meeting people and giving speeches to gain support and raise money. They spend that money on political ads that help them get the attention of the public.

Candidates for governor need to show state residents they are the right person to lead the state. This means they need to show how they will improve people's lives if they are elected. If a new candidate is trying to beat an **incumbent**, he or she may have to explain what's wrong with how the current governor is running the state. Many governors support issues that are important to voters. Sometimes a single issue—such as helping the poor or an opinion about an important bill or law—can make the difference in an election.

Not all governors hold a position in public office before being elected. Some work as lawyers, while others have been college presidents or even farmers! One famous example of someone with an interesting path to the governor's office is Arnold Schwarzenegger. The Austrian-born actor and bodybuilder served as governor of California from 2003 to 2011. Schwarzenegger was elected after Gray Davis lost a **recall election**.

Former governor of New York David Patterson is an example of a lieutenant governor who rose to the top office in the state.

Walking in the Governor's Shoes

Not all states have working lieutenant governors. Arizona does not have a lieutenant governor position. In West Virginia, the lieutenant governor is only an honorary title, which means it's a position without any pay or actual duties.

Some people become governor because the current one is unable to complete his or her term. Governors can resign due to problems they face in office or pressure from others. In New York, for example, lieutenant governor David Paterson became governor in 2008 after Eliot Spitzer resigned. Patterson finished Spitzer's term, remaining in the position until 2010. He did not seek reelection.

Being lieutenant governor first is often one of the best ways to become a state governor. A 2014 *Washington Post* story about governors pointed out that ten of fifty-five governors had been lieutenant governors. Out of those ten, seven took the job after the previous governor resigned.

Protests at the state capitol are a big way to show a governor your views on an issue. Just make sure he or she is in town when you protest!

CHAPTER FOUR

How You Can Get Involved

You may want to be governor of your state someday. But even before you are elected to office you can have an impact in your state. A governor's job is to serve the people of his or her state. He or she also listens to state residents to learn what they care about. You can contact your governor in a number of ways. Writing a letter or an e-mail is one way to get your voice heard. Governors and their staff always check messages from citizens, and they will often respond.

Some people **organize** letter-writing groups to send lots of messages to their governor. You can also call your governor! Every state has the governor's contact information on its website. You can use it to get in touch and let him or her know what you think. Even if you don't have any laws you want changed, you can just tell your governor you think he or she is doing a great job!

Taking a trip to the state capitol building is one way you can see the governor at work. You may be invited to speak to him or her, or other politicians. Then you can share your views on an issue or cause that is important to

E-mail is a great way to get in touch with your governor. You might even get a response!

Getting involved in your local government is a good way to stay up to date about politics and make a difference in your community.

you and your community. Many different laws are debated when the legislature is in session, and the governor often speaks to the legislature as well. Many people also visit their state's capital to **protest** with groups in front of the capitol building. Traveling to Albany, Des Moines, or the capital of your own state is a great way to show your governor and other state politicians that you care about the decisions they make.

Getting involved in government on any level is a great way to start working your way to the governor's office. You can write letters or e-mails to other politicians, meet with your mayor, or attend city council meetings. Discover what issues interest you. Find out ways you can help fix problems in your city or town. Lots of governors first entered politics on a local level. They learned the best ways to serve the people they represented.

It may be hard to imagine just one person making a difference in government, but don't give up! It's possible! Speak your mind, stay involved, and one day you might be standing in a governor's shoes—your own!

Get Involved!

Your governor may visit your hometown to give a speech or talk to people about different issues. Be sure to check his or her online schedule often. You'll want to be there when the governor stops in your hometown!

appoint   To offer someone a position of power.

association   A group of people who work together to achieve a certain task.

campaign   A series of actions meant to achieve a common goal.

constitution   A piece of writing that lays out the laws of a state.

Declaration of Independence   The document written in 1776 establishing the thirteen colonies as their own nation, free and separate from Great Britain.

federal   A central government that gives power to other, more local, bodies.

incumbent   The current holder of an office or position.

influence   The act or power of producing an effect indirectly without the use of force.

legislature   An organized body of people who make laws.

GLOSSARY

mansion   A very large home.

organize   To put in order.

protest   A complaint or display to show you don't agree with something.

recall election   A direct removal of someone from office by the people before their term in office has ended.

represent   To serve in place of someone.

veto   To prevent the passage of a law.

FIND OUT MORE!

BOOKS

Burke, Melissa Blackwell. *What Does a Governor Do?* Boston: Houghton Mifflin, 2005.

Harris, Nancy. *What's a Governor?* Chicago: Heinemann Library, 2008.

Jakubiak, David J. *What Does a Governor Do?* New York: PowerKids Press, 2010.

Manning, Jack. *The State Governor.* North Mankato, MN: Capstone Press, 2015.

WEBSITES

Contact Your State Governor
usa.gov/Contact/Governors.shtml

Current Governors
nga.org/cms/governors/bios

State Government
usa.gov/Agencies/State-and-Territories.shtml

MEET THE AUTHOR

Ryan Nagelhout is a children's author and freelance writer who lives in Niagara Falls, New York. Ryan has written hundreds of books, specializing in sports and Thomas Paine. His favorite is about his childhood hero, Boston Red Sox designated hitter David Ortiz. A former newspaper reporter in Niagara Falls, he enjoys board games and bowling with friends.

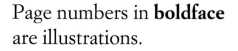